A Sanctuary Built of Words:

Poems of Peace, Grief, and Passion

by Melora Johnson

Melora Johnson
— 2018 —

Author's Note

These poems were written over the past twenty years. I hope you find some comfort or thoughts that speak to you in them.

I would like to thank my husband for his patience and understanding while I put this book together, as well as all the time he makes it possible for me to have for writing.

I would also like to thank the Corning Area Writer's Group, members past and present, for their support, encouragement, and editorial suggestions. I will be forever grateful to them.

I would especially like to acknowledge and thank my beta readers for their encouragement and gentle corrections.

Joan Cerio
Joseph Gary Crance
Carissa Lovgren
Lisa Nichols
Mattea Orr
Tarren Young

Table of Contents

No Instructions

Life doesn't provide
thick black lines to color within.
A blank canvas is all you get,
with no instructions on where to begin.

Life is no paint by numbers
with lovely watercolors and a brush;
it's a child's toy requiring assembly,
instructions thrown away in the rush.

A Sanctuary Built of Words

What if sanctuary isn't always a physical place?
Sometimes it's located in our heads; and *sometimes*
sanctuary can be found in the stories we share.

Whether our own or the ones we create, they say . . .
you are not alone - in how you *think,* in how you *feel.*

Middle of the night, middle of nowhere truths,
wisdom of our experiences, fears, and hopes,
books we shove into someone's hand –
I laughed, I cried, you must read this!
Or the ones we share through tears –
I have been through this too.

Stories say there is *nothing* you can go through
that someone,
somewhere,
hasn't been through before.

I imagine a person who comes across my words
and the problems they have,
for a little while,
seem to fade.
We connect across time and space —
a glimmer of hope and grace.

Stories create connection,
encourage kindness and compassion.

So many live in fear these days,
internalized and returned to the world
as anger and hate.

Growing up stories gave me an escape.
I know I'm not the only one who ever ran away
by stepping into the pages
of a fictional world.
People do it every day.

But it's not just about alternate worlds.
Sometimes the words of one person's existence
reach out, offer a hand – solace, comfort, hope –
to a suffering soul – keep the weary moving
forward,
peering around the next corner.

I posted an essay online once and received
two emails, anonymous, they spoke –
"I was going to commit suicide tonight . . ."
"My wife and I had agreed, but . . ."
Your words stopped me.

The words might be written last week or last year,
passed on by a friend or found on a shelf.
It doesn't matter how,
what matters is the connection *building*
until we are a chain of people,
linked through all time and space.

Holding Space

Speak to me
of your anxieties.
You don't always
have to be
so positive,
the strong one.
Give voice to your pain
and let me
gather it up,
hold it for you a while,
as best I can.
Then rest,
as best you can,
even if you don't sleep.
I will hold you
in my thoughts.

Whither Are You Bound?

Indulge, for a moment, if you will,
this woman who is feeling old today.
A bit of advice - forget your age
from time to time
and reckon your course by the stars
as they did in days of yore,
without these printed maps
in three tone color,
or directions from Mapquest,
or the GPS that says,
You have passed your destination.
Simply close your eyes and feel
the moonlight upon your face
and the trade winds in your sails.
Wither are you bound . . . today?

Sinking or Swimming?

There's another kind of fighting,
besides fighting for your life.
There's fighting for the life
you want to have . . . and live.
And there's a difference
between believing that
impossible things can happen
and believing the things
we may think impossible
might just come to pass.
I believe in riding the wave
of a benevolent universe, I said.
He scoffed as if that were silly,
some little girl's optimistic fantasy.
But surfing's not a passive sport,
and it's not for the faint of heart.
You have to know what you want.
Then you have to prepare, and wait,
always scanning the water,
watching the horizon,
waiting for that wave to come along.
It takes patience and strength
to tread water for that long,
even sitting on a board
because when the wave comes,
you have to catch it.

Dormant

Driving East on 86
in the mid-morning fog –
dark outlines of trees
stretch out their fingers
into the white mist.
Below lies a carpet
of golden brown
dormant grass.
Strange to realize
it's not really dead,
just waiting for
an awakening.

April Countryside

Gray April skies shower an inconsistent drip.
Follow a winding ribbon of gray
up the hill then down as it drops away.
Matted yellow grass, freed from blankets of snow,
fills the pasture, greening at water's edge.
Last year's corn stubble dots the muddy field,
and bare limbs move restlessly as
clinging dried orange leaves shudder-shake.
Outbuildings stand slant-sided,
unable to resist the ravages of winter
while, older still, a barn that could
squats solidly in the middle of a field.

Ruth

I knew a lady from an antique land –
Butte, Montana, in the nineteen-twenties.
She was well over six feet when she'd stand,
but always spoke with a voice low and sweet
as, with a gleam in her eye, she'd oft repeat,
"I ran my stepfather out of the house
with a cast iron fry pan at sixteen,
he was never again heard from or seen."

She'd tell me how her mother sailed alone,
Norway to America, at fifteen
or how she herself got on a bus East
the same day she graduated high school.
She loved to just sit and stare at the sky,
picking animals from clouds floating by.

How the Sky Looks Today

You know, the truth is,
I haven't really looked up.
I've looked at the scenery –
the surroundings –
the bare dark limbs of trees,
the green bushes and grass,
the bright white glow of snow,
gray at the edges with grit
as it melts into a rivulet,
trickling into the gutter.
I've seen its reflection
on the wet pavement
and in store windows.
I've felt the warmth
though my coat and sweater,
but I haven't *seen* the sun.

Keuka

The moisture in the air
blowing across her skin
was . . . *delicious*
and brought to mind silent lake depths.

A large body of water,
conjured by imagination and memory,
spreads gray and flat
beneath a blanket of early morning mist,
wreathed by trees and shrubs
along the shore.
No beaches here, just an old
broken down dock, jutting out
into the murky depths.
Silt-filled water
with tangled weeds
that grab at legs
and little fish that swim . . .

"Here ya go!"

She opened her eyes to a cinnamon latte
when what she really longed for
was more time to explore.

Sparrow Haiku

Sparrows seeking seeds
cannot conceive of wood bench
for human leisure.

A Call From Childhood

Early morning birdsong
on the first day
of daylight saving time
declares it Spring,
though the air is cold
and it is only mid-March.
What do they sing of?
Are they declaring their
sovereign ownership of land?
Is it a dating game?
Or are they giving thanks
for the bird seed we've put out?
I don't even know which bird it is,
but I recognize the call
from my childhood –
of days rising early
to walk up town streets
into the cold country air.

Agnostic Blessing

The other day
a red-tailed hawk
flew down the hill to greet me.
He banked right 'round a copse of trees
and flew low, preceding me up the drive.
He circled right around the yard,
then left around the barn
until lost from sight.
A strange coincidence, I thought . . .
but I don't believe in them.

Do I need to understand,
in order to accept, the blessing grace
of a young bear's black hair
glistening in the mid-afternoon sun?
Or the haunting stare of a wolf
who crossed my path not long ago?
No, I am comfortable
not knowing.

Hopscotching Through Memories

Hopscotching through memories of this house –
goldfinches cling to tall grass, gone to seed.
Red-tailed hawks wheel high in the sky o'erhead.
One such flies down the hill to greet me,
turns into the road ahead and proceeds
up the drive, circling away toward the barn.
Robin red breasts pop-hop across the lawn.
Near-sighted black-capped chickadees
flit through my deer blind and perch on the rail.
Hummingbirds buzz about my head
and knock at the window when the feeder's low.
Scarlet cardinal attacks his window twin,
amusing the cat peering from within.

Farther back, in my memory files,
along a trout stream with my father,
a blue heron, more white than blue,
flies along the water, legs trailing below,
its raucous cries prehistorically awful.
And, one year, eight nests materialized
in a tree down an old dirt road,
birds gone the next year,
leaving the lane . . .
strangely quiet.

Natural Systems

A bare tree stands in relief
against the mist and clouds
on a rainy ice slicked morn.
Its limbs spread out,
looking for all the world
like branching nerves
mapped out in the human form.
Nature, reflected over and
over again, in myriad ways,
demonstrates how connected
all of us are, in this robust
yet delicately balanced system.

A Fall Sunday at Home

Fall blew in on a Northern wind
and made himself at home.

Take a hot shower, hot chocolate . . .
hot water bottle under the blankets in bed.

Morning dawns, I'm cozy and warm.
Dip a toe into the cool pool of air and pull back,
shivering.

Wood warms a body three times
he says as he heads out, ax in hand –
Once in the cutting
Once in the stacking
The third time as it burns.

Hot soup on the table when he returns home,
pulling my warm hands to his freezing cheeks.

I listen to *Prairie Home Companion* as I clean,
Ostroushko's mandolin, melancholy
flowing from its strings.

Relax with a mystery book in hand,
snuggled up on the couch under an afghan.

Night falls early, dark skies clear,
all warmth races away into the stratosphere.

My Favorite Month

Can I just take a moment
to tell you how much I love fall?
The exquisite colors that settle over all
the trees and bushes, flared to life
in golden tones and scarlet hues –
the crisp air invigorates.
I shiver, even now, in this dead summer heat,
just looking at pictures of russet colored leaves,
dreaming of cool walks in the woods,
thick fuzzy sweaters, and crackling fires.
The orange of ripe pumpkins dotting a field,
fluttering corn stalks edging the cleared,
painted faces on scarecrow decorations –
Halloween brings out the little candy ghouls.
I can't wait to see smoke rising from chimneys,
smell it mix with the sweet apples and cider.
October is clearly my favorite month –
how could it be any other?

A Little Rumble

The biggest earthquake
I ever heard –
I can't remember the year,
but it was early morning
when the house started to shake.
It was nothing new.
We lived about a block
from the railroad tracks
though no train was in view.
It felt a little different though –
a little more definite,
rumbled on a little too long.
But, no cause for alarm,
except to the china figurine
who fell and fractured her arm.

Struck

Rain
Lightning
Thunder
Zap!
Sizzle.
Bright light
behind my eyes.
What happened?
Why do I feel . . .
so *dry*?

Post Tornado Dream

It moves in slow motion
but at the speed of sound
erasing my body, wiping it away,
before my mind can shut down.
Though my body feels no pain,
my sadness is infinite,
I lay in utter despair.
My child is gone. I am dying
and there is absolutely
nothing that can be done.

Spare Rooms

My favorite rooms
are on the North side
of the house.
I wonder why that is?
Perhaps because
they aren't where we live.
They've always been
colder, quieter,
a spare bedroom – the parlor,
shaded by trees.
A place of respite.
Now I escape there
to write, sometimes.
They are attached,
and yet, they feel remote.
I've imagined spirits
of my ancestors
inhabiting this space,
offering comfort
in trying times
like a buffering embrace.

Summer Nights Down Home

As a tired child, long ago,
in my grandmother's kitchen,
adult conversation
wafted over my head.
The summer night came in
with moth wings buzzing at the screen,
seeking a light nearer than the moon.
Crickets and peepers sang a lullaby
in swampy grass nearby
while coyotes yipped a chorus
in the woods beneath a darkening sky.
I walked out with my father,
his cigarette tip glowing briefly
as we watched the fireflies
sail a zigzag path
under the apple trees
out onto a sea of grass,
reflecting diamond dust
scattered across the sky.
What will my daughter know
of this place, down home?
I hope she will have the perfume
of a warm nighttime breeze
and cold morning dew in the grass
washing her feet.
More than this, I will not ask.

Almost Out of Sight

Parents are so much further
around the curve
of this road we call life.
There's not much time
for understanding each other,
for making amends,
for simply loving one another.
There's not always time
to take the long road home.

My October Meditation

Child colors a page and sings to herself
while I sit, staring out my kitchen window.
Morning coffee warms my hands
after a day of constant gray rain.
Orange and brown bat wing leaves
flutter upon a skeleton of limbs.
I watch for one to just let go and fly
against a bright but patchy blue-white sky.

Almost a year since my father died,
with so much living in between,
punctuated by still more deaths –
aunt, friend, and one not yet begun.
But here I sit and do not weep
with miles to go before I sleep.

Breathe

When it hurts the most,
just like a physical pain,
keep on breathing through.

Blues Note

Some days I find it difficult
just remembering to breathe.
The day begins and ends
on a deep Blues note.
In between –
the melody carries on
with a melancholy beat.

Like a Stone Kicked from a Cliff

What is it that brings me crashing
down, like a stone kicked from a cliff?
Yesterday I wrote twelve pages at a clip,
in between all the things a wife and mother
is called upon to do, but even still
today I wrote another few,
in between cooking and paying bills.
Yesterday I was fair nigh giddy
but tonight I feel not gay or witty.
Where did it all go?

Cruise Control

Feeling tumbled and bruised,
want to close my eyes and rest
but I'm the one driving
this beat up mess.
Crank up the tunes
and turn on the cruise;
we'll let life drive itself
while we cut loose.

Dark Terrain

This terrain is not unfamiliar,
a fog-filled road I've driven
  . . . a *thousand* times.
I can navigate here.

I reached out a hand but
didn't mean to drag you down,
or to make him cry.
Dark and twisty synapses –
is it just me or women in general?
Maybe men are the weak ones.

Feisty little old lady says,
You got your muscles?
Yes, ma'am.
She smiles. *Then I got your back.*
Reminds me, *we chose to be here*
and we'll only have to come back.

Fortune cookie slip in my pocket
from God only knows when –
Success is getting up
one more time than you fall down.

Baseline test – I can laugh
and there is still color in my world.

Sensitive

A glance, a shrug, a sigh . . .
an offhand remark skirting by.
The ramifications can shatter the Earth
or merely leave one pummeled and shy.

Scrumbling Up Meanings

I have slid into the land
of might-have-beens
and once-upon-a-times.
I look in the mirror and see,
not the one I want to be,
but a stranger looking back at me.
Whose flesh is this?
Where have I gone,
and why aren't I here with me?
I'm playing with words,
scrumbling up meanings.
Does it communicate what I intend
or merely obfuscate my feelings?

Useless

Antiques and clutter –
an old rocking chair, broken,
beautiful things that have no use.
These feelings of failure and inadequacy
from years of being picked on
and emotionally abused.
How do I get rid of those?
Better to give it all way
to someone who can fix it,
than to let it lie, dusty and unused.

Cycles of Deprivation and Denial

I am my own ghost, inhabiting this life,
adrift in the world, unseen and unheard.
Though people walk by, day after day,
they never notice the pain in my eyes.

I am . . . *unwarmed* by the sun.

Whipped, beaten, and pummeled by life.
I feel weak and small and scared,
and it makes me angry
because I used to like myself.

I used to think I was capable;
but they have trampled all over that
and made me doubt my own worth,
torn me down, bit by bit.

Living in cycles of deprivation and denial,
I need you to remind me of who I am
but you don't even see
that anything is wrong

I am unfocused and confused,
hobbled by kryptonite of some soul-sucking kind.
I bleed from somewhere deep inside,
ceding my power to this modern life.

96,000 miles per hour, spinning through space,
hurtling towards no destination
but in an elliptical motion we journey on.
How can we not come unglued at times?

It's hard to let yourself dream, or even hope,
when what you want most
always seems just beyond your reach –
always the consolation prize.

I turn to something bigger –
music feeds my soul, reconnects me to my center
and to the spheres as they orbit around the sun.
Finally, I feel the power that flows in me again.

Existential Bathtub Conversations

Existential bathtub conversation
with my six-year-old . . .
Mommy, what was Agent God in the minus one?
Somehow I feel this conversation is beyond my ken.
Oh, tough one, I don't know.
splash *Then just say Shopkins.*
Really? A cheap commercial plastic toy?
That just feels wrong but, *Okay.*
That's not the answer, she informs me.
That's only the answer if you don't know.
Ah, I still don't know, but . . .
somehow I feel better about it now.

Reality and Perception

Reality is ninety percent perception,
I'm told, but there must be
some kind of objective truth.
What *really* happened?
Can we ever find out
when experiences
are filtered through layers
of pain and doubt?
People twist and spin,
dancing around the truth,
afraid of the mirror it carries.
What are the facts?
What are the motivations?
Actions can be cataloged,
words verified, but motivations
will be categorically denied.

Rhythms

There is a rhythm that is felt
and a rhythm that is heard
and what is heard . . . can be
felt as well. Music of our souls.

Think of a ticking alarm clock
wrapped up in towels and
placed in a box with kittens
to mimic mama's heartbeat
so she can get some peace.

When you hear the sound
of a person's heart beating
through a stethoscope,
does it sound familiar?
It doesn't to me.

Oh, but that first sounding
of baby's fast-paced heart flutter
like the pitter-pat of little feet
is . . . *enchanting*.
So alien and yet so lovely,
like a recording of whale song —
an ocean with Jacques Cousteau.
That this little alien *lives* in water
and breathes . . . how?
Inside you for nine months.

The sway of a woman's step
sometimes exaggerated when
she carries a baby within,
creates a rhythm,
a dance all its own –
degenerating into a waddle
on her tired and swollen feet,
as she waits to greet the child
she has carried all these months.

We weren't even really trying
but when you *want* to get pregnant,
when all the women in your family
want you to get pregnant,
most especially your daughter,
wants you to get pregnant . . .
each monthly flow
can sweep you away
on a tide of woe.

Barriers

I still carry anger, I'll admit.
It's hard to forgive someone
who won't acknowledge regret.
The doctor warned him
as we sat there together.
He asked if I'd ever been diagnosed
with depression. *Not really,*
I said, *only because of the thyroid.*
The doctor turned to him, *Then
it's up to you to pay attention
and watch over her, for any sign.*
Fast forward a year, tears
streaming down my face,
Why are you crying now? he scorned
I don't know. Still I sobbed.
He looked at me so cold, then turned
away, carrying the baby with him.
I felt so lost inside myself.
The doctor who delivered my baby
had told me the shower was a good place
to cry, so as not to scare the family.
But what if I scared myself?
I'm still scared, of getting pregnant.
What if it happens again?
What if it's worse?
I can kind of understand that
he was scared too, didn't know
what to do, though

he'd been warned, and I can
sort of, accept that
he's the steady one,
day in, day out -
doing the dishes, taking out
the garbage, vacuuming
while I'm the one who handles crises –
when the child cries in the night,
when she locked herself in her room,
when a tornado hit the house . . .
when I lost another child.
But if I handle the crises
who handles me
when I'm the one in crisis?

Flight Risk

I was thinking this morning
how easy it would be
to just unplug from reality –
delete my Facebook account,
change my phone number,
resign from my job, walk out.
Just give up and disengage –
head West into the plains
or disappear into the mountains.
But I could not leave my child,
nor take her from her father.

Mama's Lament

Just after midnight
small heels beat a
Morse code of defiance
into the mattress –
I am not tired.
I will not sleep.
Even though
mere moments before,
or perhaps after,
chubby cheeks and hands
folded in repose
on mama's lap
angelically spoke of
sweet dreams.
Oh, but what transpires
between the rocker
and the crib?
Eyes and mouth
pop open!
Screams or laughter,
legs kick.
I am not tired!
I will not sleep!
Mama returns
to the rocker,
her weary vigil
to keep.

With a Heavy Heart

Lao Tzu said – at the center
of your being, you have
the answer, you know
who you are, and you know
what you want.
But what if you can't have it?
What if it's a will-o-the-wisp,
constantly beyond your reach?
Instead, you have obligations to keep.
Be wary of those claiming
they've come to set you free.
They may just set you adrift
without so much as an oar at sea.

Serenity or Bust

There's no reasoning with love
when it hits you.
It doesn't fix a thing.
I'll make no pretense of understanding –
love is a mystery with so many plot twists
that I may never reach the end.
Is it merely chemistry?
Or a sign of something deeper?
Of souls that have known each other
from a different time or place?
Love is chemical and physical –
it's emotional and spiritual.
It can transcend time,
making moments over into an eternity.

Might-have-beens litter my brainscape.
Not so many, really . . . just a few,
bouncing back and forth
like the numbers of a combination lock
until a click echoes through.

Is there room for more than one?
Surely.
Can your heart expand?
It must.
But culture dictates a role to play —
serenity or bust.

The Law of Attraction

I can still hear her Belgian accent —
"The erotic frisson of a kiss
that is merely imagined,
can be . . . as powerful as . . .
hours of lovemaking."
Oh . . . how I agree.
There is a mental . . .
emotional . . .
spiritual . . .
component to attraction
that transcends the physical.
It may start with a pretty face
but is unlikely to linger if
the mind is empty . . .
or the spirit corrupt.
Finding someone attractive
and being attracted to them
is not really the same thing.
Where does attraction truly reside?
In the landscape of the mind.

*This poem was first published in *The Sexuality Poems,* Foothills Publishing, 2017.

*Quote from Esther Perel's TED Talk, *Rethinking Infidelity.*

Shattered

I wasn't tongue-tied,
there were whole dictionaries
of words I longed to say,
but the timing wasn't right,
so I held my tongue
and left you in peace.
I just hope it wasn't pieces,
because I was shattered.

Missed Opportunities

Do you know the little death
of one who moves away
and is no longer in your presence?
You are gone from me,
I no longer feel your energy.
I torture myself with
glimpses of my memories
though I know those times
cannot return.
I want to hold you,
for the first time,
to kiss your lips,
in spiritus,
mingling of our souls.
Why didn't I, when you were here?
More the fool am I, fearing
to make a mistake, to alienate
when you would always go,
are going, have gone,
slipping away . . .
like a thief in the night
with part of my heart.

Au revoir

I can only pray that someday
we'll share the same space again.
I'll finally get to touch your face
and hold your hand but, perhaps
you'd shy away? I don't want you,
if you don't feel the same.
You were too much for me,
but it hasn't changed my mind,
I still love you.
So I'll watch you live your life,
love you from afar.
It doesn't make sense, and I
don't know what to do about it.
Did you feel it too, like a rip in time?
Or was I just deluding myself,
reading false meanings
into parsed lines?
I know that, with the way
this old world turns, I'll probably
never see you again, but
that thought is intolerable,
so I'll just say au revoir,
maybe someday, because I love you.
I can't conceive of saying good-bye.

Hidden

My favorite hiding place?
Do you mean –
when I was a child?
Or as an adult?
I could say, in your eyes
but really, it's in your heart.

Unrequited

Why am I still
expending so much energy
trying to comprehend
the unfathomable ways
of my very human heart?
I love him, it says,
but what good is that?
Does it help him
in some small way?
Would it, could it,
if he even knew?
Does he know?
Does he care?
Did he ever?
And does it mean . . .
anything?
Or is it just
the human condition?
Was there a reason?
Does it
help him
in some
small
way?

A Residue Remains

I love you...

Not with the passionate intensity
of the match that *flares* to life
then burns quickly down
scorching the fingertips
before being dropped
and skittering away
in a sudden gust . . .

but rather, with the slow intensity
of the quietly burning candle
that melts and drips
minute by minute,
hour by hour,
reforming itself
into a pool of rippled wax.

Even when scraped away,
a residue remains.

Controlled Burn

I've been called placid but I crave passion.
Keep the drama on the page, I tell myself,
but I want to set it *all* on fire.
Like a rocket on reentry,
I need to burn off extra fuel.
Is someone assigned for controlled burns
on the thickets of deadwood in my mind?
Sometimes I feel like an old haunted house,
infested with memories and decay.
Go ahead and burn me down;
I'll rebuild . . . someday.

Touch-me-not

I identify with
orange Touch-me-nots
that burst and split their skin,
writhing in orgasmic ecstasy,
when touched by a human hand.

For the Phat Girlz

There are guys who won't even see you
as human . . . because you're fat.
Then there are guys who will accept you
as a friend . . . but not essentially female.
There are guys who will really like you
but . . . just can't *get past* . . . it.
There are guys who will prefer you
that way, more to push and pull.
Then there are guys
who will fall in love with you,
and take you *any* way they can get you
because *you* are incredible.
Hold out for that.
'Til death do us part,
unless you get sick . . . or fat,
is just pain deferred.
When he holds your face in his hands
and kisses your lips as if
you are a work of art,
and would do anything for you,
for your pleasure . . .
hold out for that.

The Book of Love

I hear no one can read the damned thing.
It's all squiggles and dots, filled
with portents and confusing signs -
supposedly full of wise old sayings
that sound good but aren't really useful
when you're down in it, mired in the mud.
A fortune cookie might be just as good.
"Love will come to you . . .
when you least expect it."
"The one you are thinking of . . .
is thinking of you too."
"It is easier to move two mountains . . .
than to bring two hearts together."
"Cheese is good."
Things like that.

We just have to feel our way through,
lead with emotions and try not to
lose our minds along the way.
It's not always easy to do
what's best for everyone involved.
Shot through the heart.
She did it for love,
they claimed.
Really?
Probably not.
Sounds more like
a case of homicidal rage.

Sweet Summertime

C and F met in the sweet summertime;
they were young and sharp.
They fell in love, hearts soaring with the score,
but like notes in a syncopated jazz song,
they were never quite in step.
When the music ended, their love fell flat.

Time, Free Will, and our Monomyth

What is reality? What is time?
And just how are they related?
Einstein, Feynman, Hawking . . .
Who was, is, will be . . . talking?
What was and is, always will be,
but what about what will be?
Is it happening concurrently?
Have I slipped this
time stream unaware?
Is that why I loved you?
The first time I saw you,
I kept thinking that I knew you,
though it was not possible.
Was it inevitable?
Had it already happened?
It must have . . . because it did.
Did I really have a choice?
Is free will the illusion
that gives us a voice?
I can't be fatalistic,
it simply isn't in my nature,
nor my nurture, it would seem.
How was/is my life decided?
Are all my circuits firing
along predetermined paths?
Or are they creating new
pathways to a future
as yet unknown?

The future seems in flux
but maybe we're all just
taking part in one long play
where the parts have
already been written . . . by us.
We're all part of an unbreakable chain –
cause and effect, joy and pain.
Good and bad, it's fifty-fifty, but
I believe little is destined to happen
that we cannot affect.
So I'll keep striving for the good
and see if we can't make
the Universe tip its' scales.

Soul Mates

Like two souls tethered
by a long red string,
I see you out there.

Do you see me?

Regrets: A Confessional Villanelle

I'll never regret feelings in my heart.
Sometimes careless words do, in haste, slip out.
There's not much, but I do regret that part.

Standing up for myself was not my art.
More likely, in private, to weep it out.
I'll never regret feelings in my heart.

One day, untrue words were thrown like darts,
when a younger girl, hurt herself, lashed out.
There's not much, but I do regret that part.

Confessions can bring about a fresh start.
I make no claim to being a girl scout.
I'll never regret feelings in my heart.

Cruel words found their mark on a sister's heart
when I told words an unkind friend spoke out.
There's not much, but I do regret that part.

Falling for a married man wasn't smart.
A position we did nothing about.
I'll never regret feelings in my heart.
There's not much, but I do regret that part.

No Apologies

Resting bitch face,
sharp edges made up.
Is anything flawless?
Let reality be reality.
Fuck them . . .
I was built to last.
Do what you want.
Love who you love.
Be who you are –
no apologies.
Laugh at it *all*.
Let *them* adjust.

Brazen

Take it off,
take it all off,
but not for them –
do it for yourself.
Unwrap the outer edges
of your brain, leave
the trappings of society
on the floor, behind.
Show them what you're made of,
don't hide a thing.

Wild Woman, Mystic, Sage

I feel too much —
passion screaming through my head.
It's why I don't do drugs,
why I love to drink
but I've never been drunk.
I've spoken my heart
and gotten those looks that say
there's something wrong with you.
It's why I sing at the top of my lungs
flying down the highway.
I've got to get it out!
It's why I write.
I make people nervous
'til I question whether I'm sane
and tamp it down again
hiding who I am,
limit myself to make them comfortable.
Behave properly - polite, meek little librarian.
I know it peeks through,
I was born in the year of the tiger
but what can you do?
Wild animals get euthanized.
Can't lose control, have to keep it caged
but part of me screams to get out
so I bleed onto the page
and hope they don't notice
the words are red.

Don't pull your punches, Ducky said,
but even he didn't know what was in my head.
Wild woman, mystic, sage.
Wise woman, I've been called,
but I hide in this age.
It isn't safe to let it out to play
or they'll put *me* in a cage.

80s Child

Oh, my Gawd!
Blast straight out of
my 80s childhood past —
I Want My Mtv they sing.
Just like the old teen zines,
huge hair teased with spray.
Max Headroom, before true VR.
Crazy times – Challenger fell,
but I watched the Berlin wall fall too.
It wasn't all good
and it wasn't all bad,
my childhood.
I wonder if my parents
had fatalistic feelings
about the future for us all,
or were they optimistic?
The *Future's So Bright,*
I Gotta Wear Shades . . .

Playground Equipment

We didn't have that many options.
There were giant swings –
tall metal Vs that held
recycled tire rubber seats,
strong on long thick chains
and merry-go-rounds
on a hot black asphalt round,
we would cling to as
one of us raced
to get it whipping around,
before too many got hurt.
Wood chips replaced the asphalt.
Then they were just torn out.
There were giant tractor tires,
in a pyramid, where wasps lived,
and we hid, to tell our secrets and giggle.
I never liked the monkey bars
or the jungle gyms.

Considering the Fourth of July

As innocent children we ran,
with sparklers sizzling in the dark
beneath outspread apple tree limbs,
little caring why we celebrated.

Perhaps with some vague notion that
a piece of paper had been signed
long ago, like a birth certificate,
declaring our Independence.

All we cared for were the fireworks
shooting across the sky, parades,
grilled hot dogs and sweet apple pie,
and perhaps asserting our right to stay up late.

As weary adults we hope that
life, liberty and the pursuit
of happiness, is still out there,
not just a disenfranchised dream.

All men are created equal,
that's only self-evident, and
endowed by their creator with
certain inalienable rights.

We had no idea the weight
inequalities can carry
or the savage force with which
we could, would, see them come crashing down.
Now we hold our children closer
and wonder at politicians.
Do they really comprehend what lies
in the balance between promises?

We celebrate with gratitude
the sacrifices that were made,
in our Forefathers' distant time,
hoping we need never do the same.

I Weep for this World

I weep for this world,
turned upside down,
trying to shove us back into
a plasticine womb from the fifties.
We won't go . . . can't go.
America was not always great
for all those who loved her.
She could be an abusive mother
poisoned by the powerful fists
and twisted words of
an uncivil head of house.
Poor, black, gay, female or others,
unwilling to pull the yoke assigned,
suffered under her confused and drunken rages.
Sober up - lift the veil - see for once . . .
we are all brothers and sisters.
We must stand together.
There is so much
yet to be done.

Antipolarizing Lens

"If you're not with us,
you're against us."
No, nope, not anymore…
I won't be a party
to this polarizing talk.
I want to see
this country unite
for longer than the week
after a natural disaster.
There is no "them" and "we,"
there is only us, humanity.
Who are . . . *they*?
Are we really so different?
I just can't fathom it.
Or are we being played?
I've had an epiphany
I beg you . . .
reject this polarization.
When we do,
there's so much more to say.

My Facebook Feed

My head hurts from a cold that lingers
and the recriminations of a tiny person
who cannot express herself sufficiently.
Are any of us so very different?

So much I should be doing –
I am tired and I sit.

My Facebook feed today shares —

Outrage once again for Trayvon Martin.
Outrage, finally, for a woman given
20 years for firing shots meant to warn.
Outrage over the chemicals in our foods
and a missing warning on an anti-inflammatory drug.
Two separate ATV crashes killed man and woman.
A friend mourned a fellow motorcyclist.
Many remembrances of a woman who had passed –
friend, wife, mother, aunt, sister – so much to all.

Birthdays, memes, encouragement and humor
seem outweighed by outrage and pain.

At lunch today, the profound climate change came up.
North pole has packed up and moved but why?
No one denied it, no one sought to place blame.
Yet the oil industry almost seeks to hasten it.

Has the world gone mad?

Or did becoming an adult
and parent, simply wake me up?

Injustices and perplexities confound me.
Frivolities… taste stale and unprofitable.

A fortune cookie today admonished me –
When up and down seem impossible,
try moving side to side.

Outrage, outrage, outrage
must be combated by humor and art.

There is a long view out my front porch
a tar road, a green field, trees, a hill and
blue skies reaching up to into white clouds,
lilting sideways.

But what?

She walked into the kitchen
and stopped. Something,
something had changed.
She didn't know what.
There were no signs
of a struggle in flour or dust,
no knocked over chairs,
or anything left dangling.
There wasn't even a note.
The refrigerator still hummed.
The clock still ticked.
Nevertheless . . .
something had changed.
But what?

Doomed to Repeat

"This is not your mother's childhood,"
my daughter said, sitting up in bed,
one early summer night.
"It's your grandmother's."
No terrible surprise, relief in fact,
but what, precisely, did it mean?
Are we mythical archetypes
first dreamt of around fires,
cast forward through time?
Do we repeat our lives
like lines in a Petrarchan play?
Are we patterns and grooves
etched into an old phonograph?
Or echoes of radio broadcasts
. . . floating in space . . .
until they bounce back on a wave?
Maybe we're a living memory,
the hard drive of this planet,
information encoded in our DNA.
We zip around the surface of this orb
like ones and zeroes on a circuit board.
Some bits flip and some persist.
Is this what we are?

Filtered

The lights on my oven vent hood
began to flash, not regularly,
but as if to levels of human speech,
until I asked it to stop.
Each night it happens again.
My husband says, *It only
happens when you're here.*
I fancied someone visiting;
my 7-year-old scoffed.
Perhaps it's grandpa, I said.
    No, it's not Grandpa.
Perhaps it's Great-Grandma?
    No, it's not Great-Grandma.
Perhaps it's my friend Michael?
    Who is he? she asked.
He wrote poetry.
    It might be him, she replied.

Sticky Keys

Rigoberta Menchu has
been on my mind of late
though I couldn't tell you why.
No, not the author, nor her works.
Simply the *name*
has usurped my circuits
and asserted itself in my brain.
Is it a virus in the system?
Should I wipe the hard drive clean?
Or simply reboot with coffee
or a glass of wine?
Perhaps a little down time,
an update with some friends
will clear my mind.

Sleepless Meanderings

Can't sleep.
Sweet smell of hay,
first cutting of the season,
raked in the hot sun yesterday,
and cool damp air,
drift in at the window.
Wander downstairs.
Last of the coconut flour brownies.
Dishwasher running quietly.

Why do I smell cat puke?

Remind me not to walk around
barefoot in the dark at night.

Leafing

It's touching me!
It's holding on to me.
It won't let me go.
It has all of us.
Help!
Oh, my god, what
are we gonna do?
Hey, hey, you!
 I call to the leaf
next to me, but
he just flutters away.
I begin to feel
my strength ebbing.
The tree . . .
that tree!
It was stealing
the force that
infused us,
made us green,
and vital!
One by one,
we shrivel up
until it finally . . .
lets us go.
Good-bye,
cruel world,
good-bye.

Snow Day Indulgence

Today I indulged
sweet and savory, both sides,
with buttery perfect eggs
quickly scrambled
on a hot cast iron pan
while another, smaller,
heated two maple sausage links
'til they sizzled,
a cup of orange juice in hand.
Devoured, still I was not content –
combined a handful of toasted pecans,
some whipping cream and
orange cranberry, chopped,
into a mousse of sorts, then
coffee, dark roast with vanilla
and a sprinkle of cinnamon.
At last, sated, I began to write.

I Have to Write

My brain won't play poker,
it isn't kosher.
Why won't it do as it's told?
Where have all the ducks gone?
Where are the honey bees?
And where are the Monarchs going?
Twenty watts of power
can't energize a city block
but I'm not a dim bulb.
New thoughts are simply out of stock.
In the grand scheme of things,
the chance of being a new Shakespeare
or another Charles Dickens
are null and void.
It's okay, I don't want to be.
I just want to write short stories.
Well, novels, mostly.
But to do that
I have to sell a lot of books.
No, I have to convince an editor to publish me.
Or perhaps, first, an agent to represent.
Well, I have to submit first.
Really, I have to finish editing.
And before even that,
I have to write.
Always, I have to write.
No matter what else there is in life,
I have to write.

Time or Money

Would that I could manage my time
in some more productive way,
but for all that I'm doing,
I'm really doing okay.
I've amassed a wealth of words
in stories, poems, and in my head.
Someday I'll sell them all . . .
and have more time instead.

99133275R00057

Made in the USA
Columbia, SC
09 July 2018